Praise for *Losers*

'Josh Cohen has made perhaps the most pernicious, offensive and distracting word in the English language of amazing and illuminating interest. This is a remarkable and clarifying book.' **Adam Phillips**

'With compassion, skill and verve, Josh Cohen eloquently dismantles societal and personal delusions about winning and losing.' **Deborah Levy**

'Eloquent, urgent, this breath-taking essay, bristles with wit and analytic understanding. Our social settlements, our lying politicians, our very language of winners and losers has never undergone this kind of rigorous dissection before. A tour de force – or should I say a loser's triumph...' **Lisa Appignanesi**

'A profound meditation and an ethical salve for a world that wounds us with its increasing ethos of success-at-any-cost. With gentleness, Josh Cohen guides us through the paradoxes of humility, uncertainty, neutrality, and the excess of shame and humiliation that lurks behind today's peculiar brand of triumphalism.' **Jamieson Webster**

A catalogue record for this book is available
from the British Library.

First published in 2021 by **Peninsula Press**

400 Kingsland Road

E8 4AA

London

peninsulapress.co.uk

Printed in Great Britain by CPI Group (UK) Ltd, Croydon

2 4 6 8 10 9 7 5 3 1

ISBN-13: 9781999922344

Losers
Josh Cohen

Ⱶ
PENINSULA PRESS, LONDON
POCKET ESSAYS

On the eve of the Day of Atonement, the rabbi walks into his empty synagogue and ascends the *bimah*, or central platform. Overtaken by fear and trembling at the prospect of soon having to account for his soul before God, he drops to his knees, raises his arms and visage to heaven and cries out, 'My God! I am nothing! I am NOTHING!'

At this very moment, the cantor walks in. Overwhelmed by the rabbi's display of spontaneous devotion, he follows him to the *bimah*, drops down behind him and bellows in his resounding *basso profundo*, 'My God! *I* am nothing, *I* am nothing!'

Unbeknownst to both men, the beadle has been concealed at the back witnessing their abjections before the Holy One. Unable to contain his emotion a moment longer, he rushes to the *bimah*, falls prostrate behind the cantor and in his grating high-pitched squeal declares, 'My God! *I, I* am nothing, *I* am NOTHING!'

At which point the rabbi raises his eyebrow and leaning in to the cantor with a sneer and a thumb pointed at the beadle grunts, 'Huh! Look who thinks he's nothing...'

I heard this justly famous Jewish joke a good many times as a child at the family table, and it made me laugh out loud long before I got the punchline. Getting it has made the joke timelier, if not funnier. It's hard to imagine a sharper condensation of our political moment, with its rhetoric of cynically competitive humility: the vituperation of elites and experts, the promise to speak for you, the hardworking family, the left-behind, the silent majority. The joke, of course, is that the performance of humility conceals an exercise in rivalry and arrogant self-regard. Even our shared nullity before God has a hierarchy, and only those at its bottom end are naïve or dumb enough to imagine otherwise.

Look who thinks he's nothing. Yes, God finally makes losers of us all but come on! In everything there are winners and losers, so why not in losing? It feels like a good question to put to a public world dominated, until recently, by the noise of one man who could not contemplate losing even when losing, because that would make him a loser.

In fact, it was at the very moment he was made a loser that the Trumpian project revealed itself as a personal mission to deny the possibility of loss. If he lost, he repeatedly assured the world in the months before the election, it could only ever be evidence that he'd won, a prediction handily confirmed by the result.

'I do have much more humility than people would think', Trump told an interviewer in 2016. He wasn't going to show it, he added, because he wanted to remain unpredictable. Humility was a secret resource best preserved by keeping it entirely concealed. Let people know just how much humility you have, and some loser like the beadle is bound to fall under the illusion he's the same as you.

The last decade has seen the ascendancy of a politics formed by wishes, bent on expunging the presence of loss from public discourse. It declares victory over the pandemic even as countless lives and incomes are lost to it; it sells the irreversible losses of national wealth, influence and prestige inflicted by Brexit as an overwhelming win.

Being a psychoanalyst, I find this wishful politics makes me think irresistibly of another, much older region of human life built around the extirpation of loss. When Freud called the unconscious 'timeless' (*Zeitlos*), he was referring not to its universality but to the absence in it of any notion of time, and therefore of loss. This is a feature illustrated by the 'borrowed kettle' joke he liked to quote: B accuses A of having damaged the kettle he borrowed from him; A replies that it was damaged when he borrowed it, that he returned it undamaged, and that he never borrowed the kettle in the first place.

In waking life, these options cancel one another out; in a time-bound universe, a kettle cannot be both damaged and undamaged, nor can you return a kettle you never borrowed.

But in the timeless unconscious, where a thing can indeed both be and not be, such logical scruples are swept away. In its wishful confines, one need never reckon with loss, other than as a kind of furtive gain. How did it take Trump to see how effective a logic this might be for the conduct of politics, to discover that the machinations of the inner life could model the conduct of external life? You incited an insurrection, say his accusers. No, he replies, you incited it, they did it of their own volition, and in any case there was no insurrection.

Trump, it now turns out, was the rabbi, for whom being nothing is only ever another way of being everything. What if, within post-Trump world, the task of democrats and ordinary citizens still nostalgically attached to notions of truth and justice is to reckon with being the beadle, dumb enough to think that losing really means losing?

The pandemic may not have helped in this task, putting us as it has in close contact with the wish to be rabbi not beadle, the canny operator for whom losing a job and income is merely an opportunity to retool and acquire a string of marketable new skills, who will emerge from the depredations of lockdown super-fit, polyglot and proficient in carpentry.

Surely the horror of losing, in life and politics alike, arises from the irremediable certainty that we will all, albeit in varying quantities and at varying speeds, lose the things we most want: youth, beauty, love, status, money, memory, life itself (and this last in exactly equal quantity)? Coming into the world helpless and consigned to mortality, human beings might be expected to find their ethical and emotional home in humility. But as the joke reminds us, however much we may want to be humble, few of us really want to feel humbled, and least of all when we say we do. We hate losers because we are born to lose.

The problem, at least in part, may be that we think of losing purely in the negative. 'Winning may not be everything, but losing isn't anything', laments Charlie Brown, modelling a depressive submission to an order of value in which only success has substance. And yet who better reminds us how much substance there is in losing, how emotionally and existentially rich an experience it can be? My life-long love for the round-headed kid has something to do with his refusal or inability to game his compulsion to lose. Not for him the rabbi's ruse in which losing turns out to be quite something after all. Beyond a little masochistic gratification, Charlie Brown wrests no surreptitious gains from losing. And yet he's not quite the beadle either, desperate to ingratiate himself with the big nothings up there. In the absence of any elegant way around it, he instead turns losing into a total existential commitment.

The boy who compulsively surrenders his kite to a tree that eats it, courts humiliation and severe back injury failing to kick a football, who bears the insults of other children and the cosmos and his own dog with gentle and persistent *amor fati*, in whom is concentrated the childhood of every great literary loser who preceded and follows him; who better to usher us into an *art of losing?*

I see myself in my twilit years, long after the planet has been renamed Google Earth and lockdown has become a synonym for life, recalling psychoanalytic work in the age of Covid-19, and it strikes me that it will be the glitches I'll recall above all, the lags and freezes, the signal jams and exhausted bandwidth laying waste the reliability of the clinical setting.

The British psychoanalyst Wilfred Bion described the psychoanalytic session as a meeting of 'two rather frightened people'. He was referring to the discomfiting experience of contact with the unconscious, both one's own and someone else's. As he saw better than most, one of the problems of psychoanalytic work is that it can conjure away this fear too quickly. Routine wears it away, the rhythm of the work seeping osmotically into the body memories of analyst and patient, so that what initially seemed ineluctably strange – lying down in the presence of a near stranger and simply speaking – soon becomes all too familiar.

Bion's psychoanalytic pair are frightened because they are subject to the unpredictable and volatile play of their feelings towards themselves and one another. Speaking and listening to the inner life is a risky business. Unbearably violent or tender feelings can spring up as if from nowhere, rendering patient or analyst barely recognizable to themselves.

This may seem very odd, until we remember that people tend to come to analysis struggling to bear the weight and quantity of loss life is daily piling on them – of youth, say, or love or aspiration or selfhood or happiness or the will to live. Psychoanalysis asks us to remain in this state of loss, to keep feeling the painful scratch of what we lack. Why wouldn't we feel overwhelming hate for the figure who won't let us forget just how much at a loss we are, and overwhelming love for the figure who quietly endures it with us? And how could the analyst, herself no less subject to loss, avoid being caught in the contagion of these same feelings? In one way or another, everyone I work with brings me up close to losses I've once felt, or still feel or have yet to feel, provoking intense rushes of gratitude and resentment.

But because this contagion is the substance of the analyst's daily life, she's especially prone to the illusion of acquired immunity. She imagines that her patient may be frightened, but not her, not after all these years. No, she assures herself; she knows all about loss now.

The Zoom consulting room brought me a renewed awareness of my patient and me as two rather frightened people. The vagaries of teleconferencing quickly undid the consulting room's atmosphere of quiet receptivity. It turns out that the fitful clockwork motion of a buffering icon isn't really a 'waiting room', that a meaningful silence can be difficult to distinguish from a loss of signal, that the words I'd have spoken into a receptive pause in the here and now of a shared room were liable, in the two second delay time of Zoom, to cut clumsily into the patient's flow of speech.

Zoom analysis, and the virus that made it necessary, reminded me that I'm still one of these rather frightened people, scared of what I might lose. The virus had rendered me all too human, closing my consulting room to protect my own health as well as my patients', whose anxieties over their own and the world's future were self-evidently mine too. In this regard at least, it was a powerful confirmation of a basic and unpleasant psychoanalytic insight: we cannot be immunised against our own vulnerability. It seems apposite that the remote platforms that host our sessions should have become erratic and unreliable, that the stability of the analytic setting should have been put in doubt.

Yet Zoom also reminded me that analysis unfolds in the faltering, stumbling movements of language, the medium in which loss becomes perceptible. Not since my first weeks as a trainee analyst had I felt more painfully alive to words as a host for gaps, haunted by what they conceal or fail to say.

Insufficient bandwidth will often mean that a mouth on Zoom forms its words a second or two after they've been spoken, or that it's still moving even as the voice has settled into silence. This delay was a disconcertingly effective dramatization of a basic and easily overlooked truth of analysis and of life, that we never coincide with our own words, even and especially when we seem fully in charge of them.

'Every time we speak', says the French writer Maurice Blanchot, 'we make words into monsters with two faces', and nowhere is this truth more evident than in psychoanalytic work, in which both speaking and listening are under constant suspicion of duplicity and confusion. The Zoom screen has been a very effective reminder of this predicament, of the monstrous ambiguity that comes into play as soon as one person opens their ear to another.

To speak in our own voice, for psychoanalysis, is to discover an irremediable gap in our self-knowledge. The very process of trying to understand and make ourselves understood brings me up again and again before that kernel of my inner life that can't be shared or understood, least of all by me, and above all when I'm unwittingly exposing it in spite of myself.

Who hasn't stood or sat in a room with a bunch of strangers, friends even, and felt the sheer terror of saying something, the ever-imminent risk of sounding stupid or uninteresting or desperate? This is surely why so many millions take refuge in the invisible, unaccountable regions of internet speech.

In Book 2 of *The Republic*, Plato has Glaucon put to Socrates the cynical argument that the secret motive for justice is the fear of shame, of what others might say about us if we were exposed as a thief or liar. In Glaucon's telling, Gyges, shepherd to the King of Lydia, stumbles on the corpse of a former king in the aftermath of an earthquake, prises a gold ring off his finger, and quickly discovers its power to make him invisible. Were we to enjoy this advantage, Glaucon contends, we would use it to similarly unjust ends. Freed from the inhibitions of being seen and judged, even the hitherto virtuous man would yield to the temptation to steal, rape or murder 'and in all respects be like a God among men.'

But Glaucon goes further: if we knew a wearer of the ring to have maintained the same moral restraint when invisible as when visible, we would justly subject him to a kind of shame in reverse; he would be felt by his fellow men 'to be a most wretched idiot', or in a more familiar idiom, a loser. For what is a loser if not one who knowingly renounces his own advantage, who consents to have less when he could take more without penalty or cost?

Could we find a more perfect confirmation of Glaucon's proto-Nietzschean view of morality as the dubious fruit of the judging gaze of others than in the phenomenon of the internet troll? As long as we have to speak in our own name, we will be held accountable for the cruelty or stupidity or crassness of our words. Exposed to the judging gaze of others, we're at risk of feeling like losers as soon as we open our mouth.

The internet frees us from that gaze, enabling us to live in a world in which everyone else is the loser, where the inner racists and incels can reverse their imagined humiliations and enjoy the free space denied by the external world to assault, violate and terrorize their unsuspecting victims. Relieved of the burden of being himself, the troll revels in the unanswerable power of being anyone, or no one.

Of course, for the average troll this level of invulnerability remains the most fragile illusion, belied by the precarious darkness in which he hides his sadism. The web is replete with viral videos in which trolls are identified and unmasked, turning their grandiose triumph into humiliating exposure. It turns out that unlike Gyges, the troll isn't actually invisible, merely concealed.

Trump's masterstroke was to pre-empt this exposure, to invert the troll's furtive shame in his cruelty, which becomes instead an occasion for brazen pride and self-display. He made real what the troll had only dreamed of, the possibility of speaking from the Olympian heights of pathological certainty and triumphal mockery, of liberation from vulnerability to our own speech.

It may be helpful to return to Bion here, and a distinction he makes between truth and lie. Truth, he writes, has an existence independent of the thinker; it persists whether a given mind discovers it or not, such that 'the thinker is of no consequence to the truth'.

This asymmetrical relationship between thinker and truth explains the venerable affinity between philosophy and humility. To seek after truth is to know that you depend on it more than it depends on you. The philosopher may love (*philo-*) wisdom (*sophia*) but wisdom will never love her back. The dubious comfort of the lie for the thinker, in contrast, is that it's entirely dependent on him. Truth doesn't need a teller, but a lie needs an inventor.

The same distinction is implicit in psycho-analysis, between what I consciously say (and perhaps even believe) about myself and what my unconscious lets slip about me. In revealing things I don't know or don't want to know about myself (my incestuous desire, for example, or murderousness or envy), my unconscious is liable to surprise and even humiliate me. This is why the psychoanalytic pair are bound to be 'frightened people'. They are sitting in a room with truths and selves they don't know, waiting for them to spring the next surprise.

Trump embodied the fantasy of overcoming this risk of self-exposure, of forging a speech in which nothing can be heard other than what I wish to be heard. It is the liar's speech in Bion's sense, a confection originated by and entirely dependent on my conscious will. Because it has eliminated all those elements of myself and of the world that I don't know or control, it is exemplarily violent speech.

Once I acknowledge the existence of a truth that doesn't depend on me, whatever I say is provisional and uncertain. The liar's speech triumphs over that uncertainty, bringing into being a world of his own creation, modelled on his own wish rather than on truth.

This, as Masha Gessen has shown so forcefully, is what renders fact-checkers so hopelessly impotent in the face of Trump's lies. The fact-checker begins from the premise of a shared reality governed by the broad acceptance of universal criteria for truth and falsehood. The problem with the Trumpian lie is that rather than partake of this shared reality, it creates an entirely different one. Its purpose is not to challenge an existing view or assert another one, but to perform the right to impose (and revoke) any reality I choose: 'It is the lie of the bigger kid', writes Gessen, 'who took your hat and is wearing it – while denying that he took it. There is no defence against this lie because the point of the lie is to assert power, to show, "I can say what I want when I want to."'

The fact-checker, on this analogy, is the smaller kid whose tearful insistence that it's *his* hat only fuels the bully's pleasure and his own humiliation. Our shared reality is stolen from us, and its daylight robbers point gleefully at the losers who protest.

It's hard to imagine a more instantly recognizable verbal and vocal signature, ordinarily a signifier of an authentic selfhood, than Trump's. And it's odd that a speech style so evocative of a child's in its repetitive phrasing, wayward logic and disordered syntax and grammar should be so thoroughly unendearing. Unlike the child or the Zoom mouth, Trump's juddery, broken speech manages somehow to lack the smallest intimation of vulnerability, as though its secret aim were to offend language itself, to make words merely another occasion for a public exhibition of contempt.

A style of speech, elegant or clumsy, sparkling or dull, should have the effect of revealing the speaker, bringing to light the substance of his character. The intriguing paradox of Trump's singular speech is that it expresses instead a radical hollowness of self. 'A life spent entirely in public ... becomes, as we would say, shallow', writes Hannah Arendt in *The Human Condition*. The full realization of selfhood requires recognition of the boundary between the private and the public. Private space, physical and psychic, is the primary source of our depth of being.

Speculating publicly on dating his daughter, shooting random bystanders and suspending the democratic process, Trump is the apogee of the modern process, identified by Arendt, of 'the utter extinction of the very difference between the private and public realms.' In Trump, the incestuous and murderous wishes that surreptitiously shape human desire, that for most of us remain locked in the black box of the unconscious, become so much interchangeable fodder for casual broadcast.

Trump thus holds up the fantasy of total invulnerability to one's own unconscious, a kind of breezy dominion over his psyche ensuring he can say what he wants when he wants to, that if there are any frightened people (or as the popular phrase has it, 'adults') in the room, he won't be one of them. Given his compulsive visibility, Trump may seem an unlikely candidate for a present-day Gyges. But perhaps the difference is only superficial, for Trump's visibility has the same function as Gyges' invisibility – a total immunity to shame and internal disturbance, an incapacity to be surprised or humbled by the perverse and violent impulses we all harbour. Most of us instinctively hide these impulses in the darkness of our private self, shielding them from the gaze of others and so making us vulnerable to exposure. Displaying them in plain sight, Trump quickly inured us to their horror, so that we soon ceased to notice them.

*

Trump, like Brexit, grew from the soil of loss and humiliation. Both campaigns tapped into deep wells of resentment against the economic and cultural impacts of globalization. To those for whom globalization has meant only the chronic diminishment of prosperity, status and opportunity, it promised to reverse the inexorable tide of loss, to usher in a new era of unimagined and limitless winning: 'We're going to win so much, you're going to be sick and tired of winning', Trump proclaimed at a 2016 campaign rally in Albany.

The vapidity of that sentence conceals its insidious brilliance. Silently invoking and inverting the implied sentence, 'You're losing so much, you're sick and tired of losing', it promises, if it doesn't actually perform, an instantaneous alchemy of loss, like a Ring of Gyges that gifts immediate possession of everything we had once so impotently desired.

When our anxiety and humiliation at losing is transformed at once into the triumphal ecstasy of winning, of winning *so much*, we know what we know with a force and clarity that far exceeds anything a lamestream news network or election worker or Deep State legal officer tries to tell us.

In the juxtaposition between Trump's tweet-scream, 'I WON THE ELECTION!' and Twitter's appended labelling of the claim as 'disputed', we find a concentrated image of these incommensurable modes of knowledge and their respective fates. We might like to think that the social media platform's appeal to verifiable facts outdoes Trump's delusional rage; but Twitter's lowercase warning looks peculiarly ineffectual and shamed beneath the exclamatory assertion above, the trifling pedantry of a pointy-headed loser. You have a choice: the facts, which can easily be faked if you control the voting machines and foreign postal voters and fake news media and courts; or the knowledge which comes from inside, which is verified in the absolute certainty you feel right where you live.

A spate of recent books suggests that the rise of this affective mode of knowledge, dethroning the sovereignty of 'facts' and the authority of the official record, is a kind of revenge against the existing governmental order and its house philosophy, meritocracy. It doesn't need your 'expert' knowledge, it says; it can *feel* what's true. Economists, political scientists and philosophers sharing the same broad analysis of the current malaise, Daniel Markovitz, David Goodheart, Robert H. Frank and Michael J. Sandel have each ascribed the success of the Brexit and MAGA movements to their capacity to tap into resentments against meritocracy, the ethical undertow of liberal democracy, in all its right and left variants, in the age of globalization.

For Sandel, the remedy for what he calls 'the tyranny of merit' is an ethos of humility, an antidote to the self-satisfied dismissal of the lives and voices of globalization's losers, above all the non-college educated workers who have seen a steady diminishment (or devastation) of prosperity and status in the new global economy.

Equality of opportunity, the basic principle of meritocracy, is especially vulnerable to the Orwellian adjustment of some opportunities being more equal than others. This will be apparent to anyone who has lived among the urban middle classes and witnessed the private tutors, professional contacts, financial support and other little corruptions of meritocracy routinely extended to their children. The liberal middle classes, even the Tory party these days, are big advocates of levelling up, just as long as they can continue to find the foothold to the level up.

But it's not merely for its inevitably uneven application that Sandel rejects meritocracy. Even if we could eliminate the endless surreptitious leg-ups and nepotisms and cronyisms that corrupt it, meritocracy would still fail to yield a just social order. By placing the members of a society in permanent, anxious competition for its highest goods, meritocracy corrodes any notion of social solidarity or 'common good'. It is a system structured to engender and sustain an order of winners and losers, sponsoring 'hubris and self-congratulation' among the former and chronically low self-worth among the latter.

If we're to undo this divisive culture of triumph and humiliation, Sandel argues, we must cultivate an ethos of *humility*. Humility reminds us of the large portion of arbitrariness that determines any personal success or failure. It nurtures esteem for a given person's work in terms of its contribution to a common good rather than the personal wealth it commands and so 'points ... towards a less rancorous, more generous public life.'

To see the force of Sandel's critique, we need only glimpse the poisonous divisions in public life today, the pitting, by opportunistic politicians and shrill talk radio hosts, of immigrants against the 'traditional working class', the liberal media against 'the people'. In an atmosphere like this, each group furiously claims the paradoxical authority of the loser and ascribes all power and privilege to their imagined foe. Everyone shouts that no one is listening to them.

But what would it mean to promote humility as a public virtue? Here we run into a peculiar split in public discourse: if on the one hand social media has become the primary means for stoking toxic division and conflict, it is also the space of first choice for the rote rehearsal of unobjectionable platitudes about kindness and respect – another species of the verbal alchemy that imagines saying something makes it so.

Turning to a thinker from a quite different tradition, we discern just how much saying something can fail to make it so. In his 1978 seminar *The Neutral*, Roland Barthes suggests that forging a spirit of non-violence is at least as much a problem of language as of morality. The basic mode of language is the indicative, the statement that this is so; when I say that this tastes good or smells bad, my subjective view is asserted as a descriptive truth. Arrogance inheres in speech, which may be why so many religious traditions counsel habitual silence. The great nineteenth-century Belarusian Jewish sage Israel Kagan (known as the Chofetz Chaim, or 'Desirer of Life') preached the virtue of shutting up; to speak, he warned, is to be pulled into the immediate temptation of the 'evil tongue' or injurious speech. Words, those two-faced monsters, never say what we think they're saying. For Barthes, humility is an exemplary case in point. Citing Pascal's observation that 'Few men speak humbly of humility', he wonders whether humility isn't effectively cancelled out by the very act of speaking it. The problem is that humility is a 'negative *quantum*'; it is defined by lack – of self-regard, arrogance, pride and self-certainty. But, writes Barthes, 'this "negative" is ceaselessly "straightened up" into a positive as soon as one begins to speak: the humble, as soon as they speak, turn into the proud'.

The most famous exemplar of this predicament, of course, is Dickens' Uriah Heep, the unctuous, wheedling law clerk who hides his malignancy behind a show of "umbleness'. 'I'm so 'umble' may be one of the most famous modern examples of speech as performative contradiction; Heep effectively cancels out his claim by the very act of making it. We might want to argue that this is a matter of action rather than speech, that Heep's catchphrase is self-contradictory only because his behaviour so blatantly gives the lie to his self-description. But this is to miss the point that his speech *is* action, an unwitting disclosure of his duplicity.

In the face of Sandel's serious advocacy for the common good, Barthes' objection may seem too clever by half, meeting a substantive proposition about justice with distracting semantic pedantry. This would be a fair objection only if we thought of words as a neutral vehicle for thought rather than its very substance. 'We should be humble': in order to plead for humility, language assumes the register of pride.

The authentically humble person, on Barthes' account, is akin to the credulous wearer of Gyges' ring, discovered by his fellow men and women to have continued to behave justly even when invisible. The implication of Glaucon's mockery is that where everyone else has been behaving justly because they have no other option, this 'wretched idiot' has actively chosen to do so, even at the expense of his own untold advantage in riches and power. If invisibility is the test of the just, silence is the test of the humble. What's the point in being nothing if you can't proclaim it loudly to the heavens and whoever else is listening?

Humility lives without the protective shield of self-proclaimed goodness, declines to trade in Heepish reputational management. It is a stance, says Barthes, of '"diminutions," "inadequacies", "abstentions"'. It abstains from setting itself up as a positive agenda for behaviour or belief, sustaining life in a state of reticence and incompleteness.

Barthes' wariness is borne out by Sandel's robust prescriptions for an active ethic of humility, based on a notion of 'contributive justice', the universal recognition of every worker's contribution to the common good. He cites 'On Human Work', the 1981 Encyclical from Pope John Paul II which posits work as the means through which the human being achieves fulfilment, indeed 'becomes "more a human being". Work is the remedy for the 'fundamental human need to be needed by those with whom we share a common life'.

The identification of humanity with work immediately raises many questions, not least about the humanity of those who do not or cannot work – the incapacitated, the unwaged, the refugee. Sandel's ethic of inclusion, conferring recognition on 'ignored or unappreciated' labour, is itself premised on diminishing the humanity of the non-worker. His gesture of equalizing the contributions of the surgeon and the sanitation worker in the name of humility betrays a telling blind spot about its own exclusions.

Sandel proposes a kind of revolution in social attitudes, whereby mutual respect would be decoupled from achievement and prosperity. Given we cannot abolish outright differences of income and professional status, we can try to change the way we relate to those differences, holding all contributions to the common good in equal esteem. But how does such a proposal escape what we might call the Heep trap? How can it insure against the behind-hand snicker of 'yeah, right!' just audible behind the fine words?

The problem with attitudes is that they can always be faked. We might even say that such faking is apt to become part of the meritocratic order; few surgeons or corporate CEOs are likely to be so crass as to openly proclaim their innate superiority to sanitation workers or call-centre operators. Why not instead showcase one's admirable human sensitivity, insist that the mailroom guy and receptionist are no less important members of the company family than I am?

Lexicographers picked up this adaptation of Heepism for the social media age at the start of the previous decade, when many declared 'humblebrag', the use of humility to boost ostentation, their word of the year. The stance Sandel commends of 'There, but for the grace of God or the accident of birth, or the mystery of fate, go I' sounds suspiciously like an Instagrammable humblebrag, humility as another kind of prestige, conveniently costless to its speaker.

Spoken from the analytic couch rather than

Instagram, 'There but for the grace of God, accident or fate go I' is more likely to solicit suspicion than agreement. What is being muffled behind this loud profession of humility? This isn't a matter of unmasking of the patient's 'true' attitude of arrogance and entitlement, but a way of thinking of the route to authentic humility as running through a reckoning with that internalized meritocracy which has me forever reaching for the top spot, to which all my rivals are nothing but resented obstacles. Humility is possible only for one who has communed intimately with their own hubris.

What we might call a vigilant humility would be one that keeps watch on its liability to be hijacked by arrogance. I find one version of it in psychoanalysis, another in literature. Both, after all, are forms of insight and truth that cast perpetual suspicion on their claims to insight and truth. Precisely because she is set up by the very premise of psychoanalysis as the one who knows, the analyst must keep constant watch over her claim to know.

Barthes suggests literature inhabits the same tension. It is a language of lure, of spells cast by the invitation to listen to this story, this person, this image, this sound, this silence. And it invites its reader to doubt it, to resist its seductions, enjoy and dismiss it as mere literature: 'Writing is the very discourse that unfailingly baffles the arrogance of discourse', he suggests, not by renouncing that arrogance, but by showing us the spell it has over us. Every book is an unspeakably arrogant invitation to invest your time in reading it, and a poignantly humble admission of its own essential insubstantiality. Even the Bible is just marks on a page.

This is why Barthes' subtractive or abstemious sense of humility is more than quibbling. Before it can be an external agenda, humility must be an internal stance, wary of its own claim to speak and assert itself (and how wary should I be of my own willingness to say what 'humility must be'?), of how quickly and imperceptibly it can morph into its opposite.

Charlie Brown cries out in wordless anguish ('AUUGGH!') when he misses the football again, when his pitches are smashed into the stands again, when the tree eats his kite again. Losing is his way of life, humiliation his existential condition. Full of impotent rage, he kicks and pitches and flies the kite again. It's this very rage that conditions his unassuming gentleness; you cannot be humble before the world if you haven't felt the wish to destroy it.

*

Psychoanalysis is not a practice regularly associated with humility, and for good reason; built around the resistance of the unconscious to knowledge, it cast itself from early on as the vanquisher of this resistance, the sole means of bringing the unknowable into the light of day. And yet psychoanalysis was born in a moment of humility, in a forceful challenge to its founder's claim to be the one who knows.

In 1889 Freud was 33, an inexperienced physician who had only recently established a practice for the treatment of nervous illness. The exigencies of supporting a young family had led him to abandon a career as a laboratory researcher in neurology. He practiced the established treatments of the day, notably the so-called 'rest cure' famously rendered by Charlotte Perkins Gilman in *The Yellow Wallpaper* (1892), which consigned women to an open-ended period of near-total immobility and 'feeding', as well as a strict moratorium on mental stimulation. It is odd to think of the talking cure emerging from an effective prohibition of thought and speech.

When Freud saw Emmy von M. in spring 1889, she'd been suffering from bouts of nervous illness for some fourteen years. Stammering and tightly knitting her fidgety fingers, her neck and face jerked in convulsive spasms, while her mouth clacked compulsively. She was living in a state of frightened subjection to the torments inflicted by her own mind and body. As if confirming her fearful passivity, she readily assented to Freud's suggestion that she leave her two daughters with their governess and convalesce in a nursing home, where he would visit her daily.

Freud had been trained to see his patients as

the passive objects of his incontestable medical authority. But this authority proved all too fragile in the face of resistance to, even rebellion against his methods.

At the beginning of the treatment, Emmy is compliant enough. She assents without demur to her doctor's orders and proves 'an excellent subject for hypnotism', falling under his spell with the raising of a finger and the order to sleep. It is a near-parodic invocation of the Svengali motif, the masterful male hypnotist and his compliant female subject as the very model of power and submission.

Emmy has been raised to violently suppress her states of feeling. Hypnosis coaxes out memories from her sixth year which reveal the origins of her present-day terrors. But if Emmy's problem is her terror of her own feelings, hypnosis is a troublingly ambiguous solution. The hypnotist's orders, after all, repeat the very trauma they seek to alleviate – like Emmy's aunt, who shames her for showing fear and vulnerability, they tell her what she can and cannot think and feel.

The hubris of the hypnotist lies in his arrogation of the role of gatekeeper to the patient's mind, arbiter of what may enter and what must leave it. This monopolistic authority is loosened only when Emmy starts to 'supplement' hypnosis with conversation, 'apparently unconstrained and guided by chance.'

This free and undirected talk soon becomes an antidote to the hypnotist's monolithic authority, forcing him to submit to her demand that he listen rather than dictate to her. As he demands she answer his questions about her gastric pains, she replies 'in a definite grumbling tone that I was not to keep on asking her where this and that came from, but to let her tell me what she had to say. I fell in with this, and she went on without preface.'

From the perspective of patrician medical authority this is a serious defeat, not to say a humiliation. Tell me what I want to know, Freud demands, only to be told, No, I'll tell you what I want you to know, and if you don't like it, that's your problem. She refuses to reduce her inner life to the dimensions of a bald answer, to reduce her experiences to a facile sequence of cause and effect. In asking her where her stammer originates, Freud is raising the rather more monumental question of why she is who she is. There is, Emmy shows him, no ready answer to such a question. If he really wants to know, he will have to let her tell what she has to say.

Emmy's case points to the clinical birth of psychoanalysis as a scene of humiliation, a humiliation that is embraced for the creative possibilities it engenders. In overturning her doctor's clinical authority, Emmy makes space for the emergence of nothing less than a new mode of telling and hearing the truth, involving not simply letting the patient speak her mind, but letting her mind speak; and demanding from the listening analyst a stance of receptivity to the meandering drift of her speech, what he will describe seventeen years later as 'a surrender to his own unconscious activity.'

The humiliation of 1889, in other words, will give rise to a method of humility. More than two decades later, counselling newly qualified analysts on how to listen to their patients, Freud famously enjoins a state of 'evenly-suspended attention', an undirected alertness, a curiosity and openness unconstrained by prejudices and expectations: 'if he follows his expectations, he is in danger of never finding anything but what he already knows.'

The first rule and last rule of psychoanalytic listening is to forego the assumption that you know the meaning of what you hear. This is listening infused with a Barthesian suspicion of its own 'pride'. The analyst is never more in trouble than when she believes her listening is motivated by selfless dedication to her patient; the unconscious with which she listens is no less prone than anyone else's to distortion, error and violence. To listen as an analyst is to be alive to the irritation and boredom and envy and rivalry and disapproval stirred in her by the patient; this alone, not any wish to help, is what makes possible her benign neutrality.

If in ordinary life humility is a moral virtue, in psychoanalysis it becomes a way of speaking and listening to the truth of the human soul. Evenly-suspended attention, with its caution against finding only what we already know, is humility reborn as an epistemological stance and clinical attitude, an openness to the other's singular voice that has no choice but to grope uncertainly, to risk getting the patient wrong.

The patient's story will not be pared down to a known quantity. It introduces us to a private self irreducible to a quantifiable thing among things. Psychic truth is larger than us, which is why it frightens us. I learned this early in my own analysis, in an exchange that made me tremble with horror and joy. 'So, not *such* a nice guy after all', my analyst remarked after I'd ripped through a colleague with gleeful, gratuitous cruelty. I can hear his low and plain tone, describing rather than judging. It was and remains a wonderful and terrible moment for me, a loss and an unburdening of innocence, the gentle reflection back of a psychic messiness I had never allowed myself to recognise.

*

In 2018, Trump allegedly spurned a visit to Aisne-Marne cemetery near Paris to honour 1,800 American marines who had lost their lives in combat during the First World War, because it would have left his hair dishevelled and meant paying tribute to soldiers who, in stopping the German advance towards Paris, had failed to prevent their own deaths. 'Why should I go to that cemetery?' he allegedly said. 'It's filled with losers.'

The visit would have paid homage to the first and last human vulnerability, the fact of the mortal body. To be seen at the cemetery would have been to acknowledge his place in the category of embodied mortals, his inevitable consignment to the same path as the world's losers. Perhaps Trump's crassness conceals an uncomfortable insight: every cemetery, and therefore the rest of the world too, is indeed 'filled with losers'.

Mortality reminds us that loss is the essential currency of the self. And from the vantage-point of right-wing populism, there is no surer sign and seal of a loser than an acknowledged vulnerability. Like the less militarized lockdown protestors in the UK, the rifle-wielding militants who stormed state capitols were united in protest not so much against mandated mask-wearing and social distancing than the insinuation into public life of self-preservative fear for the vulnerable body.

'My freedom doesn't end where your fear begins' (or alternatively, 'My freedom trumps your fear'), runs the slogan, as though no freedom worth the name could allow itself to take account of another's fear, not to speak of one's own.

Human vulnerability, in short, has become the target of populist hatred; hence TRUMP 2020: FUCK YOUR FEELINGS.

In its passionate intensity, FUCK YOUR FEELINGS sounds like another performative contradiction, an ostentatious show of the very feelings it claims to reject. But there is no inconsistency here. The slogan says fuck *your* feelings. Your fear and horror and disgust, or even love, tenderness, solidarity – these show you up as weak, vulnerable to your feelings. Whereas *my* feelings of rage and hate and triumph trumpet my invulnerability.

This is an affective war pitting the inflated self-certainty of the id against the fragility of the ego. The ego, charged with navigating the self in the external world, is always facing the threat of loss; the id, reservoir of libidinal energy and voracious appetite, doesn't even know what loss means. In his fantasy of the wars he never experienced, Trump's being killed or injured or tortured is a logical impossibility. On the same logic, it turns out, so is losing an election.

As a slogan, FUCK YOUR FEELINGS bests its opponent on every score, including feeling itself. It speaks not for the elimination but for the absolutization of feeling. It drives feeling to the point of immunity to question or challenge. The slogan's speaker wins because he feels more than you, more purely, more violently, because your feelings are diluted by the doubt and ambivalence he scorns, and doubt is for losers.

The trolling and viral conspiracies and disinformation campaigns ravaging the public sphere are shock and awe tactics in a war on uncertainty, a sustained push to fuck your feelings.

Until they've reached a certain pitch of violence, feelings cannot be trusted not to waver or change. The phenomenon that bedevilled earnest liberals everywhere, the incapacity of new increments of Trumpian psychopathy, however spectacular, to move the dial on his 'base' support, had its origins here, in that verbal alchemy which turns supporters into permanent winners. All feelings allied to doubt – above all self-doubt, or what we sometimes call humility – had to be bombed into submission.

Trump is an avowedly fanatical adherent of the teachings of the pastor of his youth, Norman Vincent Peale, whose famous credo of positive thinking and the 'prosperity gospel' preaches that material success issues from the elimination of all self-doubt or 'negativity'. The truth about me, on Peale's account, is whatever I want to believe, a definition which sanctions the denial of whatever I don't want to believe.

The prosperity gospel effectively individualizes the cultural inheritance of American exceptionalism, the doctrine that the nation's inexorable enrichment in wealth and power is mandated by God. Just as the national doctrine could be used to underwrite the annihilation of the Native peoples that stood in its way, so its individualized iteration sees every political opponent as a malign impediment to an ordained destiny.

This starts to make sense of the curious phenomenon Dave Eggers observed at Trump rallies, where expressions of sclerotic rage were conveyed in an atmosphere of mutual affirmation and warmth. It is disconcerting to hear the unmistakable notes of genial laughter in the chants of 'Lock Her Up!', 'Build The Wall!', 'Send Them Back!'; but the dissonance between positivity and hate may only be apparent. If thinking is to keep out the negative, it needs all the incarcerations, walls and deportations it can muster.

At its Trumpian outer edge, positive thinking mandates war against anyone who casts doubt on my perfect self-image or the sunny future I ordain. Positive thinking, the systemic form of verbal alchemy, might be the paradigm of the speech of the liar as Bion defines it, placing truth entirely within the possession of the liar's conscious mind. The liar's speech involves the expulsion of any trace of the loser from the inner life, of any suspicion of the vulnerable human.

For the German philosopher Günther Anders (first husband of Hannah Arendt), the second half of the twentieth century was increasingly defined by this disgrace of human vulnerability. In 1956, he coined the term 'Promethean shame' to describe an emerging condition of universal embarrassment at 'having naturally grown instead of having been made'. To contemplate the perfect precision of fabricated things, he argued, is to lament the clumsiness and precariousness of biological bodily existence.

The striving to become a generalized being stems, as Anders sees it, from the shame of an obsolescent singularity and uniqueness. He relates the story of his visit to a terminally ill man in a California hospital, who tells him resignedly that his life can be neither preserved nor replaced. 'Isn't it a shame?' the man remarks. Anders glosses:

'He was thus suffering from a double feeling of inferiority: (1) that he could not be preserved like a fruit and (2) that he could not be replaced like a light bulb. For he was quite simply – and here the disgrace was undeniable – a categorically perishable individual piece', destined not to 'ascend to the Mount Olympus of manufactured goods', but to be 'plunged into the Hades of raw material.'

What for D. W. Winnicott constitutes the primary aim of psychoanalysis, namely the realization and embrace of one's own unrepeatable singularity, is felt by most of Western humanity as a humiliating disgrace, the sign and seal of the loser. Anders' 'Promethean shame' is the shame of lacking the undivided self-certainty of the machine.

The psychoanalytic self is a conflicted self, destined to both desire and its repression, to at once wanting and renouncing what it wants. During his first experience of sexual intercourse, the patient known as the Rat Man tells Freud, a thought flashed involuntarily through his breathlessly excited mind: *'I could murder my father for this!'* This little glimpse of his unconscious psychopathy plunges him into a hell of unremitting remorse and self-reproach. The unbound desire that had made him feel so good now makes him feel so bad.

In submitting to the psychoanalytic process, the Rat Man becomes the humiliated victim of a truth he can neither own nor control, which can strike him dangerously and forcefully at any moment. First lust and murderousness assail him, then guilt and shame.

FUCK YOUR FEELINGS promises that I will never be made a sucker of my own feelings and impulses like this, that I will always be their master and commander. In the new universe of liars and trolls, the only permissible feelings are those which are unassailable and sure. If your feelings are so weak and vulnerable as to make you feel bad, then fuck your feelings. Fuck your feelings and the loser in you, 'like a miracle ... will disappear'.

The troll doesn't need to believe what she says; the viral conspiracist is not concerned with the verities of his plots; the force of their feelings derives only from the imperative to win, to kill off the losers out there and, more urgently still, the loser within. When feeling becomes invulnerable to doubt or division or change, when it uncouples itself from any values or beliefs or hopes beyond the drive to win, it has become machinic. The problem for this machinic sensibility, as Anders' dying man poignantly reminds us, is that it's haunted by the very human fragility it has disavowed. When the expelled inner loser returns – say, after an election loss – the machine threatens to break down.

*

Ben Lerner's 2019 novel *The Topeka School* offers a history of this predicament. Like all his novels, it is at once a dazzling performance and a chastening deflation of the narcissism of literature, implicit in the very fact of asking someone, anyone, to read this.

The Topeka School completes a loose trilogy. It is based around Adam Gordon, a young poet and critic whose history and published writings are teasingly close to Lerner's own.

The son of a psychoanalyst couple at the local Topeka Foundation, Adam lives at an oblique angle to his town's sanctioned forms of adolescent masculinity. At once geek and jock, sensitive outsider and one of the guys, his divided masculinity is most on display as a high-level competitive debater. An activity commonly viewed as the preserve of weedy nerds, high school debate is being infiltrated by new strategies, much more congenial to masculine aggression.

The 'spread' dispenses with debate as a contest of persuasion in which each participant seeks to enlist the belief and support of the listener. It eschews the path of conveying ideas and values or arousing feelings of sympathy or righteousness. Turning debate into a conflict of quantitative force more than substantive argument, the spread is a tactic of overwhelming the opponent's capacity to process the arguments in sufficient time to respond. Adam writes of his debating partner:

> For a few seconds it sounds more or less like oratory, but soon she accelerates to

nearly unintelligible speed, pitch and volume rising; she gasps like a swimmer surfacing or maybe drowning; she is attempting to 'spread' her opponents, as her opponents will attempt to spread them in turn – that is, to make more arguments, marshal more evidence than the other team can respond to within the allotted time, the rule among serious debaters being that a 'dropped argument', no matter its quality, its content, is conceded.

The spread is a cipher of the creeping debasement of public discourse, the siphoning from speech of meaningful propositional or affective content in favour of anonymous machinic force. Its functional superiority to ordinary rhetorical appeal is that it doesn't rely on subjective metrics like the speaker's ability or the argument's truth value, which even the best efforts can't proof against losing. It trades instead on the most ruthlessly efficient way to win, which is to force the opponent's loss.

The lineaments of the internet troll are already audible in the spread. Speech is cut away not only from truth or meaning but from elegant rhetorical effect. Political debate is no longer a matter of persuasion but of quantity – the debater speaks with a speed and volume that overwhelms any attempt to process the words' content. This is language not as truth or lies but as sheer force, an instrument not of deceit but of humiliation.

Adam finds himself caught through the course of the novel between two forms of language, between words as vehicle for escalating menace, for triumph over the other in debates or trash-talking fistfights, and words as a path of hospitality to the other, as in the psychoanalytic vocation of his parents or his own poetry. In psychoanalysis and poetry, language recovers its humility, its awareness of its potential violence and duplicity.

In what turns out to be his last debate, Adam uses his concluding speech to renounce the spread, linking it to the historical moment's 'blind commitment to economic growth'; both, after all, 'depended on the belief that more is always better, accumulation at all costs.' It results in his losing; the judges decline to reward speech that questions itself and the very premises of the competition. The debate is witnessed and narrated to us by his mother, who tells of being 'moved by seeing my son defend a more human scale of exchange, by his rejection of linguistic overkill'.

This defence of language on a human scale, eschewing speech as an instrument of force, marks the beginning of an embrace of a different kind of speech on Adam's part, a more precarious speech, which remains alive to its own potential for violence, while seeking solidarity rather than triumph over its interlocutor.

*

Freud famously placed the violation of the taboo on incest at the heart of psychoanalytic thinking. Oedipus' crime in possessing his mother sexually and realizing the repressed desire of the unconscious would become Freud's model of neurotic fantasy and anxiety. In his short paper 'On Arrogance', Bion introduced a second Oedipal crime, occluded by the infamy of the first: 'the arrogance of Oedipus in vowing to lay bare the truth at no matter what cost.'

This Oedipus, victor over the Sphinx's riddle, looms larger in the unconscious of a certain class of patient than the fantasy of maternal seduction. For the borderline or psychotic patient, the tantalizing and terrifying danger of arrogance is represented by analysis itself. And such patients aren't wrong; psychoanalysis is indeed a promise of greater self-knowledge, of a new and disturbing intimacy with one's own unconscious.

This version of psychoanalysis arouses and nurtures the patient's arrogance, stirring them to a collusive triumph over the unknown regions of the psyche. It is also a betrayal of the basic Freudian premise that the unconscious resists full knowledge. And once again, it is in language that we run up against this resistance. 'Words', writes Freud in a footnote to *The Interpretation of Dreams*, 'since they are the nodal points of numerous ideas, may be regarded as predestined to ambiguity'. The fact that we all have an unconscious means that none of us are in the position to establish the precise meaning of what we or anyone else thinks or says.

We are speaking here of the charged ambiguity of emotional truth. Surely the same ambiguity cannot apply to factual truth, which must remain scrupulously neutral if it isn't to become an object of manipulation and deceit, and which must thereby place premium value on clarity and straightforwardness. This liberal faith in the incontestability of facts imagines it is fighting a heroic rear-guard action for the preservation of Truth. This is manifest in the proliferation of books and articles identifying some new culprit for the creation of a 'post-factual' world. This person often turns out to belong to the same small group of late twentieth-century French theorists, or else some more overarching movement like 'postmodernism'.

At issue for the fact-checkers battling the

onslaught of Trumpian lies is the protection of verifiable and publicly documented facts from their brazen denial and contradiction. 'Of course I love my mother!' may be an ambiguous statement; 'Donald Trump called John McCain a loser' is not. It states a truth, confirmable by reference to a public record, that no amount of obfuscation or denial can alter.

The problem here is that the fact-checker assumes Trump is fighting on his territory, as though there were competing evidential claims that could be resolved by establishing which is correct, forcing the liar's concession. But each time he presents the facts beyond dispute, he gifts Trump a new opportunity for their theatrical repudiation. The intention behind Trump's denials is not to contest the record but to perform his power to say what he wants when he wants.

Trump takes no inspiration, conscious or otherwise, from Jacques Derrida or Michel Foucault in this regard; he doesn't seek to ambiguate or cast doubt on facts, but to sweep them aside. It isn't a matter of questioning their veracity but of displaying his indifference to them.

From this perspective, the fact-checker in the post-Trump world would do better to abandon the stance of disinterested neutrality. For 'where a community has embarked upon organized lying on principle', Arendt argues, the appeal to factual truth becomes unavoidably political: 'Where everybody lies about everything of importance, the truthteller, whether he knows it or not, has begun to act; he, too, has engaged himself in political business'.

When factual truth is under siege from perpetual denial and distortion, whoever speaks for it is assigned a place willy-nilly in a political struggle. When liars preside over public life, even the most supposedly uncontentious appeal to the record becomes politically and emotionally freighted.

What Lerner sees in the spread is a cipher of this predicament. In ordinary forms of debate, agreed-upon facts are materials marshalled in the service of argument. The spread turns them into a kind of quantitative force whose purpose is not to refute opponents but to batter them into submission. The spread envisions a world in which facts have been emptied of the truth content that facilitates understanding and replaced with an overwhelming noise that blocks it.

To invoke the terms of philosopher of language J. L. Austin, the spreader transforms statements of fact from constative into performative utterances. Where the constative utterance can be fact-checked, subjected to a definitive judgement of truth or falsehood, the performative utterance is meaningful not for what it says but for what it does ('You're under arrest', 'You're fired!'). Like Trump, the spreader speaks not to make a claim but to silence his antagonist, to put a brake on their capacity to respond.

While not every performative is a lie in Bion's sense, every such lie works best as a performative. In acting rather than making a claim, the performative kills off the dimension of truth the liar cannot possess or control, creating instead a reality that bends to his dictates, that does as he says. The effect of this new reality is not only to neutralize the fact-checker but to drain emotional truth of its essential ambiguity.

Feelings, after all, are a problem for the liar. Our feelings are never under the full command of our conscious minds; this is why our facial expressions and tone of voice and chance phrasings and bodily gestures so easily betray us. We are prone to disclose what we feel in spite of ourselves.

FUCK YOUR FEELINGS offers up a violent 'no' to any such ambiguity. It is the emotional equivalent of the spread, a rejection of feeling as substance in favour of feeling as pure, furious noise. Those Trump rally slogans may be noxious, but to argue with them is to be lured into the same trap as the fact-checker. If we object that we can't lock up political opponents or deport naturalized citizens, we treat the slogans as though they were saying rather than doing something, the very mistake the kid makes when he insists the hat belongs to him.

Just as the kid fails to recognize that the bully is not arguing about the ownership of the hat but wilfully destroying the conditions for any such argument, so objections to the rally slogans miss their real intention – to fuck your feelings, to create an affective reality that is as radically undivided and incontestable as the rest of the liar's reality, where any words or thoughts unsanctioned by the Trump campaign will be overwhelmed by the raw, contentless noise of the spread.

*

But there is a peculiar division in the speech of the political liar. To the enemy who questions or challenges the lie, it returns only a screech of generic invective; to its adherents, its voice is rich in silky promises. The imminent future of greatness, or of control taken back, feeds us a vision of the Anglosphere as an expansive gated community, a soft-focus Eden of manicured suburban lawns and frolicking fair-haired children, keeping out the unwholesome intrusions of mass migration, natural disasters, pandemics and all the other avatars of the climate emergency.

In a famous late fragment, Freud noted the ego's habit of responding to the apprehension of danger by splitting itself. On one side of this split, the danger is reluctantly acknowledged so that it can be denied or disavowed on the other. The ingenuity of this solution is that it affords simultaneous protection and exemption from the lurking menace.

Splitting carves out a space in the mind in which any threat to my bodily or psychic existence can be consigned to blissful ignorance, in which nothing intrudes to spoil the pleasure of invulnerability or the invulnerability of pleasure. It affords us a permanent, unbreachable immunity to any virus, allowing us to retreat to this side of the split, where our vulnerability can be kept out of consciousness.

And it turns out that once established, this mechanism has infinite applications for the future of both individual and group. The fantasy of invulnerability is wonderfully elastic. Climate change is a Chinese hoax, there is no need to fear

Covid-19, police brutality is the over-zealousness of a few bad apples. You can congregate among the faithful and eschew the need for a mask and its implicit acknowledgement that you might be harmed or killed. Splitting preserves the happy, near-psychotic delusion of total immunity. The minor glitch in America's inexorable return to greatness has been all but eliminated.

Hence the mockery of masks and distancing as Trump strutted the stage before the close-packed, adoring crowds, inviting them to marvel at the lightning-speed recovery of a perfect physical specimen. In the atmosphere of the liar's planet, there lurks no surfeit of carbon dioxide, no structural racism, no viral droplets; lies pump the toxins out of earth, seas and sky and spray them over the other side of the wall, which the enemy seeks vainly to climb.

But what happens on the other side of the split? If the one side accommodates and protects this delusion, surely the other must acknowledge the danger's reality, however resentfully? Certainly. On the other side of the liar's idyll lurk swarms of criminal migrants, rioting crowds of leftist agitators, joyless liberal fascists and hectoring 'experts'; these are the properly real dangers, long obscured by the fake crises of climate and racial justice.

Unerring vigilance is needed to sustain an endless war against the malignant network of forces forever seeking to undo this partitioning of psychic reality, to deprive the faithful of the world they wish for. Heroic efforts have been mounted to unmask and put an end to their machinations: see Q's ongoing war against the Satanic child abusers of the Deep State and Bill Gates' secretion of mind control chips in the Covid vaccine.

Splitting is a misnomer insofar as it implies a clear opposition between conflicting positions; but the deluded idyll and the dystopic threat of the liar's imagination are the warp and weft of one fabric. The liar's reality corresponds to a region of the unconscious in which wishes are sovereign, in which there is no gap to endure between desire and its gratification, into which

the limits and frustrations of reality never obtrude
It acknowledges that reality only in the form of
its violent repudiation. It would rather kill the
messengers of the real than listen to them.

The more absolute the split, the more it kills
the possibility of humility, of receptivity to any
thoughts or feelings not our own. Humility is
the consequence of an awareness that truth
doesn't belong to us. But it's something else too:
an acknowledgement of our own susceptibility
to silencing or killing the other, the insistence
in us of the violence we disavow.

*

In his seminal 1961 book *Totality and Infinity*,
the Franco-Jewish philosopher Emmanuel
Levinas lays out the lineaments of what he
calls a fundamental ethics. This is ethics not
as a derivative branch of philosophy but as its
very ground. For Levinas, philosophy's primary
questions are to be found not in the arcane,
sealed-off speculations of metaphysics, but in

our concrete relations to other persons.

In Levinas, humility becomes the essential mood of philosophy. In opening myself to another person, and more specifically another face, I am uprooted from my secure habitation in my own self. The other's face, if I am properly receptive to it, signifies what he calls an ethical command, the absolute and irreversible priority of the other over myself. The raw vulnerability of another face suddenly and brutally rips through my being and its persistence in serving my own needs, enjoying my own pleasures.

The presence of the other is experienced by us as an involuntary self-exposure, inducing reticence and uncertainty, the humility that comes of no longer feeling in possession of oneself. Levinas associates the opposite state of cellular self-certainty with Gyges, the human being who cuts himself off at the root from all needs and demands but his own: 'Gyges is the very condition of man, the possibility of injustice and radical egoism, the possibility of accepting the rules of the game, but cheating.'

For critics such as Slavoj Žižek and Alain Badiou, Levinas' ethics is the voice of superego piety, a kind of punitive war on even minimal self-interest. There is likely some truth to this charge, but it is complicated by Levinas' awareness of the sheer insistence of selfhood in the face of the demand of the other. Gyges is not the villainous exception but 'the very condition of man'; our consignment to a single mind and body is also a chasm between oneself and the other. It is morally and psychically easier to stay inside our egoism than let it be broken open.

Part of the reason Levinas' ethics can seem so punishing is that it describes with uncanny precision the resentment and rage we feel when wrenched out of our complacent self-satisfaction. The face of suffering – the oppressed, poor and displaced, the bereaved, depressed and wounded – spoils my complacent pleasure in my own self. The merest glimpse of it can make us want to switch channels, or else stare gormlessly into the screen, barely distinguishing it from the endless flow of brief, indifferent retinal impressions. This impatience with suffering others, Levinas reminds us, is a kind of violence, the expression of a wish to annihilate those who disturb my peace.

This is why the face of the Other (the capital O indicates its ethical elevation), bearing an ethical demand that won't let me mind my own business, is a temptation to murder. And what provokes this temptation is a kind of an excess in the Other's face, an unquantifiable and elusive presence that can be neither grasped nor controlled. The sheer alterity of the face defies my power and as such is liable to drive me to rage:

> I can wish to kill only an existent absolutely independent, which exceeds my powers infinitely, and therefore does not oppose them, but paralyzes the very power of power. The Other is the sole being I can wish to kill.

My wish to kill the Other arises from precisely from her humbling of my power; the face's naked appeal resists me not because of its greater force but on the contrary because, as Levinas writes, it 'has no resistance'. This humbling, if I can surrender to it, can be an opening to the Other, a means of displacing me from the centre of myself. But for Levinas, this openness to the Other is a hair's breadth away from the rage to kill the Other.

A similar insight about the proximity of humility and violence is offered in *The Topeka School*. Lerner's novel isn't a pious tale of moral conversion; its interest is not in the triumph of good over bad speech, but in their unsettling intimacy, which comes to light in the diptych of incidents that comprise the final chapter. In the concluding scene, Adam and his family participate in a demonstration at ICE (Immigration and Customs Enforcement) against the Trump administration's caging of the children of asylum-seeking immigrants.

The book's final image is of one of the organizers speaking without the prosthesis of a microphone:

the 'human microphone', the 'people's mic', wherein those gathered around a speaker repeat what the speaker says in order to amplify a voice without permit-requiring equipment. It embarrassed me, it always had, but I forced myself to participate, to be part of a tiny public speaking, a public learning slowly how to speak again, in the middle of the spread.

To learn to speak again in the middle of the spread is overcome one's Promethean shame, the 'embarrassment' of which Adam speaks, to embrace the human voice in all its fallibility and self-doubt. Without the machinic amplification of the microphone, the public voice is carried by the solidarity of its listeners, even as the ears of the population are assailed by the unbroken shriek of the trolling machine.

But this initiation into humility is complicated by the scene that precedes it, in which Adam brings his two young daughters and elderly father to the local playground. When a boy at the top of the slide refuses to let the girls down, Adam approaches the boy's father, who aggressively rebuffs his request to come over and help. The dispute soon becomes an altercation, in which Adam mobilizes 'an element of discursive surprise: I've been trying to enlist your help, I said, leading with a Foundation [that is, Topeka Foundation] vocabulary, but delivering it as though I were talking shit.'

Channelling the language of therapeutic understanding in the service of shit-talking menace, Adam here points up the disturbing proximity of the languages of humility and violence. Draining the conciliatory vocabulary of the Foundation of its manifest content, he effectively spreads his 'bad father' opponent, who finds himself duly silenced, 'clearly startled by the mixture of passion and dispassion, the tangle of vocabularies'. But is Adam projecting into his antagonist his own startled reaction to how easily his language of humility and inclusion has morphed into one of humiliation and exclusion?

Adam is at once ruthless spreader and sensitive poet, lovingly protective father and dick-swinging alpha male. If the book's final scene sees the tentative, hopeful return of public language to the humble scale of humanity, the preceding scene has seen him cynically weaponize therapeutic language against a rival man.

The juxtaposition of scenes suggests that the passage to humility always runs through one's own violence. Humility isn't a voluntary stance of the righteous moral sensibility, as Sandel seems to suggest; it is wrested from, and requires the acknowledgement of, the will to vanquish or kill the Other, and the terror of shame and humiliation.

If humility is to be more than sentimental piety, it requires awareness of its own nearness to violence. This awareness has shaped psychoanalytic practice from its inception, as the case of Emmy von N. showed us. Emmy floods Freud with the sheer force of her suffering at the very moment he seeks to impose himself on it. Faced with this excess of the Other's pain, Freud is tempted to reimpose psychiatry's classifying discipline on his recalcitrant subject, or, put more simply, to shut her up; instead, and at her explicit demand ('let me tell what I have to say'), he consents to be the recipient of her suffering, giving birth in the process to the psychoanalytic method.

In letting Emmy tell what she has to say, Freud refuses the hypnotist's preference to nurture his patient's splits, to remove the negative from the reach of consciousness and create an internal empire of happy vibes. This is the monumental insight that the psyche is a space of ongoing conflict, in which coexist radically incompatible impulses.

This is the true significance of Oedipal desire, that rather than lying on either side of a divide in consciousness, the truth of my feelings is dispersed across it. 'I wouldn't *dream* of sleeping with my mother and killing my father' means both exactly what it says and its exact opposite. A man's parents can be the object of his conscious love and honour and of his unconscious lust and murderousness.

In a crude popular caricature of psychoanalytic thinking, the unconscious portion of these divided passions becomes the unvarnished truth, while the conscious attitude becomes its mendaciously polite cover story. But the 'yes' of the voracious id is no more or less true than the 'no' of the repressive ego. The affinity of psychoanalysis to poetry, as Adam seems to hint, lies in this intimacy of apparent opposites, the intimation of a zone of language in which the speaker might, in the words of Paul Celan, 'keep yes and no unsplit'. If either practice has any force today, it surely resides here, in its resistance to the compulsive splitting that organizes our politics and society.

Humility demands an awareness of its own hair's breadth proximity to the murderer's violence. Humility for this reason, as Barthes has already shown us, eludes every claim to have achieved it; it is the very quality that resists possession and (in Levinas' phrase) 'escapes power'.

The liar wants to purify himself of the vulnerability and uncertainty this implies. Resisting the liar cannot mean the inverse purity, a claim to be innocent of the liar's violence and self-certainty. Truth and uncertainty must be kept unsplit.

Meritocracy, as Sandel and other critics point out, ultimately satisfies almost no one. Its losers are left to carry the burden of the belief that their low status can only be a true reflection of their own capacities, while its winners are mired in the state of perpetual anxiety induced by the imperative to maintain their high status.

Perhaps this casts some light on the function of so-called positive thinking. The idea that sustained optimism, happiness and self-confidence will ensure the best outcomes is more than pop-psychological orthodoxy. Thinking positive is a central part of the neoliberal apparatus; the unemployed in the UK are required by state job centres to keep diaries of the positive actions they have taken to find work, while the corporate sector has been taken over by the exponential rise of executive coaching and the cult of the management guru. A BBC documentary, *The Call Centre*, features a manager who begins the working day with a compulsory mass sing-along, sponsored by the nostrum that 'happy people sell, miserable bastards don't'. Lest we imagine this was a mere diversionary entertainment, he tells the TV audience that he sacked two workers who declined to sing.

The logic of positive thinking tacitly coerces us into bathing the world before us in the sunlight of the fulfilled future, conjuring a kind of compulsive distraction from the darkness of the present. No one saw this coercive tendency more clearly than the mid-twentieth-century German philosopher and cultural theorist T. W. Adorno. For Adorno, the task of philosophy and art alike is to break the spell of illusion cast by such false affirmations.

In the name of this task, he adopted a technique of extreme over-statement, as though the grip of affirmative culture on the collective mind could be loosened only by radically inverting it, forcing us to see the violence lurking in its innocuous benignity. This is the running motif of *Minima*

Moralia, a remarkable collection of aphorisms, written between 1944 and 1949 in Southern Californian exile.

It's hard to read this book without seeing Adorno staring in stupefaction at the sunlit freeways of LA, the landscape of unrelieved neon affirmation. Each aphorism shocks us into discerning the horror concealed by these sunny surfaces. Remarking on 'the admonitions to be happy', he writes: 'there is a straight line of development between the gospel of happiness and the construction of camps of extermination so far off in Poland that each of our own countrymen can convince himself that he cannot hear the screams of pain.'

The shock of the insight derives from its drawing these radically opposed images into a kind of enforced intimacy. The sheer audacity, even violence, of placing the Californian smile alongside the extermination camp scream induces a kind of nervous laughter in me. It's as though Adorno is telling us how exposing an obscenity requires him to get unnervingly close to perpetrating one. There is an unmistakable violence in the comparison, but a violence aware of itself, seeking to break the spell of an unacknowledged and pervasive violence cast over us by the happiness gospel.

In fact, Adorno didn't simply dismiss happiness as an ideological delusion; in 'Resignation' a short radio talk from 1969, broadcast shortly before he died, he argued that a form of authentic happiness persists even in the reigning culture of false happiness – the happiness of thinking. 'Thought is happiness,' he concludes, 'even where it defines unhappiness: by enunciating it.'

In striving to choke off all negative feelings, we render our unhappiness more unreachable and so more irremediable; only in enunciating unhappiness are we released to the full range of affective experience and so awoken the possibility of a different state of mind.

Adorno's notion of thinking as happiness might spur us to experience differently the meritocratic binaries of winning and losing, to trouble the simplistic opposition between failure and success. He raises the provoking question whether breathing in the air of our unhappiness might not refresh rather than toxify our lungs.

In encouraging us to fixate on the win on the horizon, meritocracy keeps us in the perpetual anxiety of losing. It ensnares us in a self-defeating loop from which there is no exit; failure engenders shame, triumph anxiety. Bearing witness to this oscillation between persecution and humiliation, it's difficult not to laugh, both at and with its victim. 'Nothing', declares Nell in *Endgame* (a play about which Adorno wrote one of his finest literary essays), 'is funnier than unhappiness, I'll grant you that'.

How is it we immediately recognize the truth of Nell's remark without having to think about it? Perhaps because it comes from a region where thinking has already been forsaken, the region occupied by the great silent film comedians, who draw laughter from a single source: the compulsive iteration of the same mistake. Perhaps nothing more properly embodies humility than the funny man who makes a spectacle of his unending defeat.

Seeing someone slip on a banana skin is faintly amusing; seeing them then get up and slip on the same banana skin, say twelve times running, is pure hilarity.

There are writers who put flesh on the bone of Nell's remark, who seem to relish their immersion in the waters of unrelieved loss and failure. In Thomas Bernhard, Franz Kafka and Robert Walser, we find versions of losing that feel less like a judgement on life than a way of living and imagining the world. They ask us to listen to voices both humiliated and humbled, to embrace the laughter special to unhappiness by pushing unhappiness to its maddest outermost edge where it seems to become something else, impossible to name.

Bernhard, Kafka and Walser, German language writers from, respectively, Austria, Bohemia and Switzerland, writing out of linguistic and cultural outposts of mainland Germany, and out of existential regions radically displaced from the familiar human world. Their writings are at once intimately autobiographical and utterly distant from any life we know. Their lives are defined by physical and mental illness and long-term hospitalizations, by the impossible desire for human relationships and the equally impossible desire for self-understanding, another comically miserable predicament. Perhaps this is why they form a chain of transmission of sorts – Kafka admired his predecessor Walser, Bernhard admired them both.

I've been surprised to find reading each of these famously tormented men and their stories of pain, defeat and despair induces a peculiar happiness in me, which I suspect is an effect of what Adorno calls 'enunciating unhappiness'. Their stories of losing and humiliation offer no cheap consolation or homiletical comfort, no assurance that, as celebrities and executive coaches delight in telling us, failure is the necessary route to success. But they render their own or their characters' narcissistic agonies with a transformative intensity that neither reverses nor redeems the fact of losing but turns it instead into an imaginative resource infinitely richer than mere winning.

There are moments in listening to their plaintive ranting, wheedling, grudge-bearing and humblebragging monologues that I hear a sudden, disturbing but unmistakable echo of the former President, of his compulsive nursing of grudges, his wearisome loops of accusation and complaint, most tormentedly against those fickle allies who 'didn't do enough' to prove their fealty. The decisive difference is that the writers use words not to avenge their grievances and humiliations, to rise above them in vindictive triumph, but to stay with them, to show themselves and us the imaginative possibilities of losing. As I see it, their intimacy with the persistent temptation to bitterness and entitlement makes them far more effective diagnosticians and critics of right-wing populism than an army of liberal defenders of facts and decency.

In his 'Afterword' to Bernhard's *The Loser* (1983), the critic Mark M. Anderson stresses the neglected dimension of laughter and therefore of irony and exaggeration in Bernhard's writing. Laughter, Anderson suggests, operates as a kind of hope in Bernhard.

Plunged with each sentence into ever-deep-

ening, vertiginous spirals of despair, I experience a kind of cathartic purgation, discharged
in stupefied laughter. I ride the waves of the narrator's contempt, disgust and rage at the world and
everyone in it and can't help laughing. Bernhard's
narrator sees with pitiless clarity the duplicitous
world in which holy men compete to be nothing. And so I laugh not at him, because he isn't
laughable, nor with him, because he isn't laughing, but at how these journeys into the depths of
negativity can make me feel so alive and fearlessly
curious about the horrible feelings I harbour. In
the words of writer Ben Marcus, 'Bernhard is,
finally, uplifting and revelatory, because he does
not turn away from the most central and awful
part of reality.' Every Bernhard narrator is an adult
counterpart to Charlie Brown.

Cumulatively, these writers offer a singular
course of instruction in the art of losing. I'll begin
with Bernhard and move backward in history
through Kafka's address to the father who has
forever defeated him, to Walser's trainee in
servitude, who invites us to imagine choosing

to lose, to venture an impossible experiment in humility.

*

Gathering Evidence, Bernhard's five-volume memoir of his youth, chronicles an unrelieved catalogue of emotional abuse and physical suffering. Yet the voice that recounts his years in a predictably sadistic and negligent Hitler Youth-run boarding school in Salzburg, in the death ward of a hospital and finally at a fetid sanatorium for victims of lung disease is devoid of any trace of self-pity or sentimentality. His gaze has the forensic insight and ironic disgust of someone who has long lived on intimate terms with the worst humanity has to offer.

In his career as novelist and dramatist, this capacity to look horror and cruelty squarely in the face may have sponsored his fearless scandalizing of his fellow citizens, charging the nation with an abject and ongoing failure to work through its Nazi past and pointing out the persistence of antisemitism and petty nationalism at its very heart. He speaks, that is, from the standpoint of one who has nothing to lose only because he's already lost everything. The narrators of his novels each speak in one single, unbroken paragraph, turning over the same caustic judgements and complaints in different combinations. In the face of an unhearing addressee, you can only repeat yourself, compulsively and impotently.

Bernhard's Austria is another version of the culture that responds to horror, and especially the horror it has itself perpetrated, by spreading a fog of affirmation. Its narrator inhabits and stretches a single moment in time, his entrance into an inn in Wankham, a few miles from the hunting lodge where his friend Wertheimer, the titular loser, had lived until his recent suicide. The inn is a purgatorial den of rural kitsch, an instance of the 'gaudy new tastelessness' belied by its fetid, unventilated air and surfaces thick with accretions of grease and dirt. Here, true singularity and greatness cannot breathe for the noise and stink of ersatz demotic cheeriness;

it is just the place to host the narrator's and Wertheimer's life-stories of losing.

The Loser reads suspiciously like an experiment in imagining meritocracy at its furthest and most violent possible extreme. In their youth, the narrator and Wertheimer were among the most promising graduates in piano at the renowned Salzburg Mozarteum, where Bernhard himself trained – as an opera singer until his lungs prevented it, and eventually as an actor.

When Wertheimer and the narrator come under the tutelage of Vladimir Horowitz, their life plans are catastrophically disrupted by the arrival of a new student from Canada: Glenn Gould. No sooner do they hear Gould play than both the narrator and Wertheimer decide that his genius renders their own musical ambitions entirely redundant. In a parodic rehearsal of the compulsion to repeat, the book does little more than turn over this experience of sudden and total deflation again and again and again. The narrator won't or can't stop returning to the same scene, where in the simple act of playing a few bars of Bach, Gould sounds the death knell of his friends' careers.

Wertheimer and the narrator's response to Gould is the wild amplification of a sentiment familiar to anyone who's had anything to do with creative life, the peculiarly reflexive humility triggered by an encounter with greatness in one's own field of endeavour. A sentence of Alice Munroe's, or a trill of Alice Coltrane's, a Matisse line, a George Best dribble – you look and listen and ask yourself in melancholy wonder what on earth the point is of trying.

Yes, I speak from experience. I pick up Maurice Blanchot, say, and read this: 'in literature, deceit and mystification not only are inevitable but constitute the writer's honesty'; or this line from Winnicott: 'It is a joy to be hidden and a disaster not to be found'. These are sentences I've cited and glossed an indecent number of times over decades of teaching and writing, and that still have the power to stop me in my tracks.

They are near-miraculous condensations of worlds of thinking and practice, of work and inspiration, my awe of which can sometimes make it difficult distinguishing gratitude from resentment. It is easy enough to talk about the good days when these pages serve as a spur to better reading and thinking and writing, when I feel thankful for the glimpse of what is possible, when the humility they induce feeds my creative desire.

But there are days too when these lines can strike me rather like those few bars of Bach strike the hapless colleagues of Glenn Gould, when I feel condemned to churn out inelegant expositions of ideas whose depth and luminosity mine will never approach, when the car of my creativity has its wheel stuck in a ditch of incoherence, superficiality and pale imitation, when the common root of humility and humiliation becomes all too evident and I wonder bitterly why I bother and whether I should in all conscience continue to do so.

I do continue though, in spite of the daily reminders of being so far from best. Whereas for the narrator of *The Loser*, 'When we meet the very best, we have to give up'. Then, a few pages later, 'Glenn destroyed our piano virtuosity at a time

we still firmly believed in our piano virtuosity.'
These kinds of avowal, so typical of the Bernhard
narrator, seem like an affront to reason, the more
so on account of the iron clarity and rationality
they assume on the page. How can there not be
room for more than one kind of pianist? How
can differences in talent be deemed so absolute
and so final?

I wonder if we run up against the deep unconscious of meritocracy here. In the everyday,
waking meritocracy in which we live and work,
we assure ourselves that, after all, there must be
room for many gradations of talent, for many
levels of ambition and success and thus for
failure, frustration and disappointment, perhaps
even modest and quiet contentment with some
small share of the goods. This is what makes it
possible not to give up when we meet the very best.

But what if meritocracy were underwritten
by an unconscious Platonism, for which there is
only one true Idea, in whose light all other objects
are revealed as pale and insubstantial shadows,
mere copies and copies of copies, unworthy of

thought and attention? Isn't this the harsh and unremitting judgement cast by Glenn's bars of Bach on Wertheimer and the narrator? *When we meet the very best, we have to give up.*

Although it's worth reminding ourselves that Gould doesn't impact on the narrator in quite the same way as Wertheimer. While both submit to the judgement that after hearing him, they have no business continuing to play, the book is really about the different ways the two men live with this judgement.

This difference is sealed in the two names Glenn confers on his two friends: on Wertheimer, *the loser*, on the narrator *the philosopher*: 'Wertheimer, *the loser*, was for Glenn always busy losing, constantly losing out'. The subsequent course of Wertheimer's life bears out the observation all too accurately. Sinking into the mire of his self-pitying bitterness, he hangs himself from a tree within sight of the house his sister has moved to in the Swiss town of Zizers with her banker husband. This is supposedly Wertheimer's violently shaming and unanswerable reproach to her for abandoning him in Vienna.

But for the narrator, his sister's desertion of him is just a cowardly decoy,

> to deflect attention from the fact that nothing but Glenn's interpretation of the *Goldberg Variations* as well as his *Well- Tempered Clavier* was to blame for his suicide, as indeed for his disastrous life. But Wertheimer's disaster had already started the moment Glenn called Wertheimer *the loser*, what Wertheimer had always known Glenn said out loud, abruptly and without bias... We say a deadly word to a person and at that moment are naturally unaware that we have actually said a deadly word to him, I thought. Twenty-eight years after Glenn said to Wertheimer at the Mozarteum that he was a *loser* and twelve years after he said it to him in America, Wertheimer killed himself.

Glenn's teasing moniker is nothing less than a death sentence, albeit one to which Wertheimer has already acceded. In naming Wertheimer thus, Glenn has simply disclosed the truth already immanent in him, that he is born to lose, or put differently, that he will only ever be able to experience anything that happens to him – Glenn's brilliance, his sister's marriage, his own belated turn to the 'human sciences' – through the filter of losing. Wertheimer has destined himself to that absolutist meritocracy in which one winner floods all the losers with his shaming light.

Wertheimer's giving up the piano is only the first act in his prolonged drama of giving up on life, the first signal that anything he does, including ultimately the very act of living, must be erased. The loser must himself be lost to the world, forgotten; if the narrator is right that his sister's desertion is the red herring that diverts from the real reason for ending his life, then his suicide, too, for all its histrionic ostentation, is just another way of ensuring his true self is consigned to oblivion.

After the loss of music and his sister, we learn, Wertheimer had wanted to publish a book,

> but it never came to that, for he kept changing his manuscript, changing it so often and to such an extent that nothing was left of the manuscript, for the change in his manuscript was nothing other than the complete deletion of the manuscript, of which finally nothing remained except the title, *The Loser*.

Wertheimer's erased book is the perfect self-representation, a work emptied of all content but the title, which itself signifies the emptying of all content. But there is another book called *The Loser*, the one we're reading, which has made the hazardous journey that Wertheimer's couldn't, from the mind of the narrator to the page.

The difference between these two books is the difference between *the loser* and *the philosopher*. In identifying with the name of *loser*, Wertheimer announces that it's not merely his vocation that he gives up, but any meaningful experience of giving it up. Piano virtuosity was all, such that without it he is literally nothing. Losing can only be winning's diametric opposite, the zero to its one. There is no life that can grow from it, no book that can be written from it.

The narrator sees what Wertheimer doesn't, that losing is more than a featureless waystation on the triumphal road to winning. It is a substantive experience with a texture of its own and rewards of its own, that can give rise to a book of its own, an art of its own. To bear with losing, to find in it a special kind of imaginative resource, Bernhard suggests, is a more interesting and more difficult than simply renouncing life, either by means of the figurative exit of self-pity or the literal one of suicide.

The Loser translates the untranslatable *Der Untergeher*, more literally one who undergoes, bears, suffers. Heard in this way, the title raises the question of who is really designated by the *Untergeher*. For Wertheimer's tragedy isn't that he suffers but that he can't suffer, that he escapes life instead of bearing with it. The philosopher, on the other hand, ends the novel alone in Wertheimer's room, listening once more to Glenn's *Goldberg Variations* on Wertheimer's record player. Humbled but not destroyed, he has lost without becoming the loser.

*

It won't come as a surprise that one of the writers Bernhard most admired was Kafka, the epic prose-poet of abjection and powerlessness. *The Loser*, a story of living in the vast and unbroken shadow of a superior, can't but evoke Kafka's famous and unposted *Letter to His Father*, written in 1919 from a sanatorium in Schelesen, just four years before he died. An intricate weave of pleading and reproach, at once helplessly turbulent and artfully controlled, the *Letter* is a belated address to Hermann Kafka, father and tyrannical landlord of Franz's soul.

The shadow cast by Gould in *The Loser* is vocational, obscuring for both Wertheimer and the narrator any sense of who they are and what they should do with their lives. A similar shadow falls on the writer of the *Letter*, but its source is his own father. On first reading, Kafka seems to be writing out of Wertheimer's position, the loser in a struggle that could only ever have had one winner.

But the more closely we read it, the more the *Letter* comes to trouble any clear line of demarcation between winning and losing, to stake out a space beyond it. Franz's extreme self-abjection before his father Hermann is hedged with sly ambiguity from its beginning. Comparing the two of them, Kafka aligns himself with his maternal family, the Löwys:

> me, to put it very briefly, a Löwy with
> a certain Kafka core that is simply not
> driven by the Kafka will to live, prosper
> and conquer, but by a Löwy-like force
> that moves more secretly, more timidly,
> in a different direction, and which
> often breaks down completely. You, by
> contrast, a true Kafka in strength, health,

appetite, loudness of voice, eloquence,
self-satisfaction, worldly superiority,
stamina, presence of mind, understanding
of human nature, a certain generosity, of
course with all the faults and weaknesses
that go with these advantages, into which
you are driven by your natural disposition
and sometimes your hot temper.

We bear witness here to a kind of theatrical staging, and upstaging, of the Oedipal drama that turns its raw currents of fear and hostility between son and father into something altogether stranger and more guileful.

Casting himself in the role of loser in the struggle, the supplicant son reveals his timidity and fragility before the robustness and superiority of his father. But the long list of triumphal qualities seems by some surreptitious yet precise calculation just slightly to overplay its own hand, so that it becomes difficult to distinguish it from mockery. We soon lose any clarity, in other words, about who's really winning and who's losing.

The letter pursues the equivocal comparison as far as it will go. In the changing cubicles of the swimming baths, a scene Oedipally saturated to the point of parody, the 'puny wretch' of a boy must measure himself against the 'strong, tall, thickset' man flooding him in shadow. The account of their intellectual discussions fall into the same indistinction between awe and disdain: 'You had reached such heights, solely by your own efforts, that you had unbounded confidence in your own opinions.'

Two dramas are playing out on the same stage: in front, the fragile and timid son prostrates himself before the father's absolute power; behind, the same son exposes the cracks in that power. The imperious man-mountain in front is belied by the hot-tempered, thickset, capricious man behind.

Hermann's perpetual victory over the world around him is the effect of an incapacity to imagine any other outcome: 'You took on, for me, that enigmatic quality of all tyrants whose right to rule is founded on their identity rather than on reason.' Hermann wins only because he cannot lose.

And just as the father's façade of quasi-divine authority barely conceals a secret underbelly of childish entitlement, so the son's veneration cannot be felt apart from his contempt. Hermann's barked demands and reproaches are 'as good as God's law' for little Franz, and absurd in their grotesque inconsistency: 'At the table we were to do nothing but eat, but you cleaned and trimmed your fingernails, sharpened pencils, dug in your ears with your toothpick.'

So which of Franz's fantastical projections are we to believe, the infallible man-god or the revolting slob? The supreme father who makes and upholds the law or the inept father whose gross hypocrisy undermines it? Perhaps it's both, but even then, the possibilities bifurcate; is Kafka writing his letter out of a terror of subjection to a father so sovereign he can exempt himself from all the laws with which he demands everyone else must unfailingly comply? Or out of barely concealed derision for a father with the self-awareness and discipline of a spoiled child?

It must be symptomatic of the Cyclopic state of

mind engendered in me by long-term confinement that I can't stop reading Trumpian allegories into even the most anachronistic of texts. Then again, it was Trump that brought me to these texts, not the other way around, so perhaps it's inevitable I'd find him hiding in their corners.

At the most superficial and least consequential level: it is hard to read the letter today and not be struck between the eyes by the portrait of overbearing vulgarity, self-certainty, narcissism and cruelty.

As an autobiographical record, the *Letter* reads like an extended chronicle of losing. His unending defeat by his father has cost him his freedom, his confidence in the world and his trust in others. His self-respect, his clear conscience and successive possibilities of marriage are all laid waste by Hermann's criticism and casual contempt: 'I was no real match for you; you soon disposed of me; all that then remained was escape, bitterness, grief, inner struggle.'

But in enunciating it, this same chronicle subtly but decisively transforms Kafka's unhappiness. Writing his crushing defeat to his father becomes a means of changing it. In the very act of documenting the successive humiliations visited on him in the past, Franz gives them new meaning in the present.

What is this new meaning, if not a certain wisdom in the art of losing? In conceding total defeat on every front, Franz insinuates a new truth. Hermann may be a version of Bion's liar, for whom truth is whatever he says it is. But Franz is not the fact-checker impotently correcting him, pointing out how right I was and how wrong you were, and the *Letter* is not some righteous self-vindication after the fact. The truth of its belated riposte to Hermann is far more ambiguous: you are the tyrannical god who's ruined me and the clown no one could possibly take seriously.

The corollary of this: I am the defeated son and the writer who has survived the defeat, both loser and winner and therefore neither. There is an echo here of the first of the so-called *Zürau Aphorisms*, written just a year before the *Letter*: 'The true path is along a rope, not a rope suspended way up in the air, but rather only just over the ground.

It seems more like a tripwire than a tightrope.'

The path that carries us towards truth is also a rope that will trip us up. This is the key to what I've been calling a vigilant humility, the knowledge that the moment I assume the safety and reliability of the ground beneath me is the moment I'm most prone to trip on my own pride. The *Letter* takes care to tread this precarious path, to maintain the constant awareness that its very concession of defeat can't help being a retaliation, that the concession of a loss is liable to shade dishonestly into the claim of a win by stealth.

Perhaps this equivocation explains why it could never be sent; without an addressee who can readily read its intent, a letter is effectively nothing. The *Letter*'s fatal two-headed monstrosity was bound to consign it to the grey zone of literature. It thus leapfrogged its own destiny as a personal letter with a single addressee to become a literary work with countless readers.

Isn't this another profoundly ambiguous triumph? In the mere act of setting it down, Kafka transformed his personal grievance against his father into the general form of the literary. The one reader to whom the letter speaks directly, and to whom it appeals for recognition and response, was exchanged for an infinity of readers for whom it could only ever be an object of their intrusive fascination. The letter wins posthumous fame by remaining unposted and so renouncing its own wish for a hearing; this alone renders it a fundamental lesson in the art of losing.

*

Few comments capture more sharply the vagaries of literary fame than Robert Musil's description of Kafka as 'a peculiar case of the Walser type'. Robert Walser's reputation has long been dwarfed, humbled we might say, by the global literary juggernaut that is Kafka, a situation that, given their common quest for a state of 'infinite smallness' (Kafka), would no doubt vex the latter as much as gratify the former.

The quest for smallness is the quiet obsession of Walser's writing – the disarmingly apologetic sweetness of its voice as much as its content. His novels are peopled by young chancers and loafers assiduously dodging all opportunities to attain settled, wage-earning respectability; his unclassifiable essays an endless litany of tributes to the unnoticed and insignificant. In 'Ash, Needle, Pencil, And Match' (1915), he extols the virtues of ash, 'modesty, insignificance and worthlessness personified, and best of all, it's filled with the conviction that it's good for nothing.'

Ash, substance without substance, 'really nothing at all', dissolves the moment we try to grasp it. Why not make its radical humility a model for the human being? This is the implied question animating Walser's third novel, much admired by Kafka, *Jakob von Gunten* (1909). Informed by his own experience a few years previously of training as a servant in Berlin and working briefly as a country house butler, it takes the form of a young man's diary during his time as a student at the Institute Benjamenta, a school which trains its pupils for servitude as a means not merely to a practical vocation but to remaking their very selves.

The means and ends of this remaking are the same: humility. The Institute inverts the standard aim of an educational institution, to expand and develop the self, in favour of the ideal of total contraction of self, of becoming, as Jakob puts it, 'a charming, utterly spherical zero'. What if, the novel asks, smallness and insignificance were posited as a kind of grand ambition?

From this perspective, the place of the punitive ideal occupied by Glenn Gould in *The Loser* and by Hermann Kafka in the *Letter* is occupied by Jakob's fellow pupil Kraus, a young man identified with the state of servitude to the point where pursuing his own desire or self-interest has become literally unimaginable. It is his pure humility, his being so entirely at one with his own insignificance that renders Kraus 'so gloriously, so powerfully happy in himself'.

Kraus, reflects Jakob, is a 'deep, insoluble riddle' entrusted to the world by God. Indeed, the riddle of Kraus runs so deep that it isn't merely its solution that eludes us, but the very fact of its being a riddle:

Nobody wants to solve it, because there
isn't a person living who'll suppose
there is some task, some riddle, or a more
delicate meaning, at the back of this
nameless, inconspicuous Kraus. Kraus
is a genuine work of God, a nothing,
a servant ... Kraus, modesty itself, the
crown, the palace of humility, he will do
menial work, he can do it and he will
do it. He has no thought but to help, to
obey and to serve, and people will at
once notice and exploit this, and in this
exploiting of him lies such a radiant,
golden, divine justice, shimmering
with goodness and splendor. Yes,
Kraus is the image of legitimate being,
utterly monotonous, monosyllabic and
unambiguous being.

This passage seems like a clear instance of the
elevation of self-renunciation we find in almost
every religious confession from the Abrahamic

monotheisms to the Hindu and Buddhist traditions. But it harbours a difference, near imper-
ceptible and yet decisive. Kraus's self-nullification
isn't motivated by devotion to the glory of God
or any other higher force. A riddle can be solved
only if it conceals a meaning recognizable within
a shared symbolic reality. But Kraus is too modest
a piece of work to contain anything but his own
'unambiguous' being, unambiguous in the strict
sense that it signifies nothing but itself.

Isn't Kraus the startlingly exact inversion of
the rabbi and Uriah Heep? In the mouths of the
latter, 'nothing' or "umble' are the ultimate two-
headed monsters, their manifest self-effacement
concealing secret agendas of guile and self-
regard. Kraus is the perfect solution to this
Barthesian conundrum; if to proclaim humility
is to annul it, then humility can preserve itself
only in the state of radically unambiguous being.
And yet not even this zero-degree selfhood
entirely escapes ambiguity, for under Walser's
eye, humility starts to look like the strangest
imaginable quality, a grey zone in which the

very highest – 'radiant, golden, divine justice' – merges into indistinction with the very lowest – a 'nameless, inconspicuous ... nothing', as though divinity itself were now just a bit of flotsam drifting through time and space.

As Jakob tells it, he and his brother were born into the wealth and privilege that they now renounce. They have fallen out of any social order, any hierarchy of betters and inferiors, winners and losers. There is aspiration, even passionate aspiration, but its aim is contraction, not aggrandizement. Its aim is,

> To be small and to stay small. And if a hand, a situation, a wave were to raise me up and carry me to where I could command power and influence, I would destroy the circumstances that had favoured me, and I would hurl myself down into the humble, speechless, insignificant darkness. I can only breathe in the lower regions.

If the highest being is also nothing, then the foundations of every hierarchy come crashing down at a stroke. Jakob and his elder brother Johann laugh over a restaurant table at their shared understanding of the world as a place of corruption, in which one must aspire, 'even passionately so', in the knowledge that 'there is nothing, nothing worth aspiring to.' Which is to say it may just be worth aspiring to nothing, to the sheer superfluity of Kraus.

Following his own modest literary successes in Berlin, Walser himself seems to have destroyed the circumstances that had favoured him, to have hurled himself down into the lower regions. Having returned to Switzerland in 1913, a self-declared 'ridiculed and unsuccessful author', he had himself admitted to an asylum in 1929, having suffered years of increasing obscurity, poverty and mental deterioration. He transferred to the Herisau asylum in 1933, where he remained until his death during a long walk in a snowy wood on Christmas Day 1956.

Perhaps Herisau gave Walser the mode of life in which he could be small and stay small, an inversion of the upper regions in which he couldn't breathe. Here, greatness consists not in worldly achievement but in that which is, in Jakob's words, 'quite grey, quiet, hard and humble.' In such a world, the bully who shouts 'loser!' could only be looked at askance in confusion and pity, for he would have no place.

*

Perhaps I should give up imagining that any insight could be gained from casting Trump in the yellowed light of these sickly and disordered lives and writings. But I can't help it, can't help feeling that they each one of these weird men understand him infinitely better than a full battalion of political pundits. They would understand as so many pundits do not that Trump's defeat is not their triumph, that the rightful meritocratic order has not been magically restored.

They understand the world in which people long made to feel like losers find some semblance of meaning, love even, in the promise of a new world where losing is abolished by executive order, where, if they can just remain in his light, immunity to illness and death will be theirs too, and the fear and the masks can be left to the losers.

Those weird men, after all, knew better than most what it was to feel like a loser; they too imagined a world in which losing would be abolished. They just saw it differently, realizing you couldn't abolish losing for some but not for others; that this strategy would only divide the world once more into winners and losers. They saw that winners need losers, but that oddly the reverse doesn't apply, that, sooner or later, everyone gets to be a loser and that this is peculiarly good news, for it also means that in the end there are only losers and therefore, contra the rabbi, no losers.

Now that I've remembered it, it seems odd that I'd forgotten 'New Year's Resolution', a short story by Lydia Davis from *Samuel Johnson*

Is Indignant (2002), which reads as a kind of anxious riff on the rabbi joke. Perhaps it was a bit of unconscious spite; the story didn't acknowledge the joke, so I wouldn't acknowledge the story. But now that it comes back to me in some small flood of reparative guilt, I can't avoid it, given how acutely it spells out what's at stake in being nothing.

It replaces the clerical trio with a less hierarchical duo, the narrator and her friend Bob, whom she asks about his New Year's Resolutions. He tells her 'with a shrug', as though their unthinking genericity was self-evident, that he'd like to 'drink less', 'lose weight'. When he turns the same question on her, she doesn't feel ready to reply.

After a few days dipping into Zen texts, she decides, 'My New Year's Resolution is to learn to see myself as nothing.' Immediately she worries that next to the modest wish to lose weight, this aspiration seems jarringly competitive, not to say incompatible with the spirit of Buddhism. Yet she isn't being competitive, she insists, but humble, or at least she thinks she is: 'in fact, can anyone be truly humble at the moment they want to learn to be nothing?'

The real confusion here is that it's taken most of her life to learn to see herself as something. Now she has to reverse the process, spend the second half of her life 'learning to see [her]self as nothing. You have been a negative nothing, now you want to be a positive nothing.' And this is where it gets really difficult; no matter how close you think you get to emptying yourself, 'something' is bound to come along and start 'throwing its weight around', so that 'by evening, I'm full of something and it's often something nasty and pushy.'

Perhaps, she concludes, she needs to take this as a hint that she's overshot herself, that instead of aiming directly for nothing 'I should just try, each day, to be a little less than I usually am.'

Can anyone be truly humble at the moment they want to learn to be nothing? What formulation could better capture the moral comedy of a vigilant humility, caught in the insoluble predicament of undermining its own goal in the very fact of pursuing it? If you're not to be the 'nasty and pushy' rabbi, a self-advertisement for the world's humblest guy, what are the alternatives?

You could be the cantor, with all the obsequious envy of the sidekick, or the beadle, with all the desperation of a man unaware he long ago slid past the zero of nothing and into the red zone of negative numbers.

But the story gives us one more option, itself humble in its clear-eyed sobriety. It says that the urge to be something, to push ourselves to the fore, to indulge our greed for love and recognition, is always going to come to the surface and throw its weight around: let's try to know this about ourselves, and the urge may slowly begin to tame itself, at least a little. This isn't much, which is why it might also be the most radical imaginable prescription.

Though it might also not be. There you go: look who thinks he's a little less than he usually is.

Bibliography

Adorno, T. W., *Minima Moralia: Reflections from Damaged Life*, trans. Edmund Jephcott (London: Verso, 1985)

— 'Resignation', *Critical Models: Interventions and Catchwords*, trans. Henry Pickford (New York: Columbia University Press, 2005)

— 'Trying to Understand *Endgame*', *Notes to Literature Volume 1* (New York: Columbia University Press, 1992)

Anders, Günther, 'On Promethean Shame' reprinted in Christopher John Muller, *Prometheanism: Technology, Digital Culture and Human Obsolescence* (London: Rowman and Littlefield, 2016)

Arendt, Hannah, *The Human Condition* (New York: Doubleday Anchor, 1959)

Austin, J. L., *How to Do Things with Words* (Oxford: OUP, 1973)

Barthes, Roland, *The Neutral*, trans. Rosalind Krauss and Denis Hollier (New York: Columbia University Press, 2005)

Beckett, Samuel, *Endgame*, *The Complete Dramatic Works* (London: Faber, 2006)

Bernhard, Thomas, *The Loser*, trans. Jack Dawson, Afterword by Mark M. Anderson (London: Vintage, 1991)

—*Gathering Evidence*, trans. David McLintock (London: Vintage, 2003)

Bion, W. R., *Attention and Interpretation* (London: Karnac, 2007)

—'On Arrogance', *Second Thoughts* (London: Karnac, 2007)

Blanchot, Maurice 'Literature and the Right to Death', trans. Lydia Davis, *The Work of Fire* (Stanford: Stanford University Press, 1995)

Davis, Lydia, 'New Year's Resolution', *Samuel Johnson Is Indignant* (New York: Picador USA, 2002)

Dickens, Charles, *David Copperfield* (London: Penguin, 2004)

Freud, Sigmund, *Studies on Hysteria*, *The Standard Edition of the Psychological Works of Sigmund Freud*, trans. and ed. James Strachey, Volume II (London: Vintage, 2001)

—'The Unconscious', *Standard Edition*, Volume XII

—*The Interpretation of Dreams*, *Standard Edition*, Volume V

—*Jokes and Their Relation to the Unconscious*, *Standard Edition*, Volume VI

—'The Rat-Man', *Standard Edition*, Volume X

Gessen, Masha, *Surviving Autocracy*
(London: Granta, 2020)

Gilman, Charlotte Perkins, *The Yellow Wallpaper*
(London: Penguin, 2015)

Kafka, Franz, *Letter to His Father*, published
as *Dearest Father*, trans. Hannah and Richard
Stokes (London: Oneworld, 2008)

—*Zürau Aphorisms*, trans. Willa
and Edwin Muir and Michael Hoffman
(New York: Schocken, 2015)

Lerner, Ben, *The Topeka School*
(London: Granta, 2019)

Levinas, Emmanuel, *Totality and Infinity:
An Essay on Exteriority*, trans. Alphonso
Lingis (Pittsburgh: Duquesne University
Press, 1969)

Plato, *The Republic*, trans. Desmond Lee
(London: Penguin, 1998)

Sandel, Michael J., *The Tyranny of Merit:
What's Become of the Common Good?*
(London: Allen Lane, 2020)

Walser, Robert, *Jakob von Gunten*, trans.
Christopher Middleton (New York: NYRB
Books, 1999)

—'Ash, Needle, Pencil and Match', *Girlfriends,
Ghosts and Other Stories*, trans. Tom Whalen,
Nicole Köngeter and Annette Wiesner
(New York: NYRB Books, 2016)

Josh Cohen

Winnicott, D. W., 'Communicating and Not-Communicating Leading to a Study of Certain Opposites', *The Maturational Process and the Facilitating Environment* (London: Karnac, 2005)

Acknowledgements

Thanks to Will Rees at Peninsula for his invitation to contribute and for editing the result with such an effortlessly sharp eye for both the detail and the whole, as well as to Jake Franklin and Sam Fisher.

This was written almost entirely during lockdown, requiring an especially generous portion of Abigail Schama's love, patience and good humour. Daily lunches with our sons, Ethan, Reuben and Ira were an ever-renewable source of hilarity and one of the year's great lifelines. This book is for them.